SS 6115
(1)

CW00853229

FIRES

ANN WEIL

R.I.C. Publications®
www.ricpublications.com.au

Air disasters
Deadly storms
Earthquakes
Environmental disasters
Fires
Mountain disasters
Sea disasters
Space disasters
Terrorism
Volcanoes

First published SADDLEBACK PUBLISHING, INC.
Three Watson Irvine, CA 92618-2767
©2005 Saddleback Publishing Inc. All rights reserved.

Published under licence 2005 by R.I.C. PUBLICATIONS® PTY LTD
PO Box 332 Greenwood 6924 Western Australia
www.ricpublications.com.au

Distributed by:
Australasia
R.I.C. Publications, PO Box 332, Greenwood 6924, Western Australia
www.ricpublications.com.au
United Kingdom and Republic of Ireland
Prim-Ed Publishing, New Ross, Co. Wexford, Ireland
www.prim-ed.com

Reprinted 2008, 2013

Photo Credits: pages 38, Bettmann/Corbis

ISBN 978-1-74126-322-0
Printed in South Korea

CONTENTS

TIME LINE ▶▶▶

19 December 1974

A movie called *The towering inferno* is released about a fire in an office building.

20 July 2000

Mesa Verde National Park in Colorado closes after a wildfire grows from 20 hectares to 200 hectares in three hours.

Where is Colorado?

COLORADO

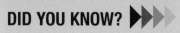
KEY TERMS ▶▶▶

wildfire

a fire that spreads very fast, making it difficult to put out

fine

to demand that someone pays money for breaking a law

inferno

intense heat

Chapter 1   Introduction

People have relied on fire for many thousands of years. Early humans used fire to warm themselves and cook their food. They also used fire to frighten away animals that might hurt them.

Fire is a basic part of modern life. People still use fire to cook and to heat their homes.

Fire can also be a killer. A house fire can turn deadly if people do not get out in time. Fires seriously burn many people. These injuries are very painful and take a long time to heal.

Every year fires destroy many homes and businesses. Fire is expensive. Fires cause more damage than floods, tornadoes and other disasters combined.

Wildfires

Toasting marshmallows and telling scary stories around a campfire is a lot of fun. But campfires can burn out of control. Wildfires destroy forests and parks. Wildfires also kill many animals.

Some wildfires are caused by lightning. Careless people are also responsible for many. Dropping a lighted cigarette outside on a hot, dry day can start a huge blaze.

Sometimes people start wildfires on purpose. They may think it's fun. But these fires are no joke. Many homes are destroyed by wildfires. Firefighters risk their lives battling them. People caught starting wildfires are fined or sent to prison.

Fires and Earthquakes

Earthquakes caused some of the worst fire disasters in history. Big cities are most at risk of fires after an earthquake.

Earthquakes damage gas lines. Gas leaks lead to explosions and fires. Earthquakes also damage water pipes. After an earthquake there may not be any water to use to fight the fires. San Francisco, California, and Tokyo, Japan, are two big cities that suffered huge fires after earthquakes.

Office Buildings on Fire

A popular disaster movie of the 1970s was called *The towering inferno.* It was about a fire in a high-rise office building.

Office buildings have safety features to protect people from fire. Sprinklers are designed to turn on automatically. Water sprays over a fire to put it out. There are usually fire escapes and fire stairs so people can leave a burning building quickly.

When terrorists crashed two planes into the World Trade Centre, the jet fuel exploded and set the twin towers on fire. This real-life towering inferno was the worst fire disaster ever.

The first full-time fire brigades were started back in the 1800s. Firefighters today are well trained and highly skilled. They use modern equipment to control fires that threaten lives and destroy property.

Wildfire, Summer 2000

Summer, 2000, was the worst wildfire season in the USA in the past 50 years. Hot, dry weather in the western states was mostly to blame. By the end of August, 74 180 fires had burnt more than 2 600 000 hectares across the United States.

DATAFILE

TIME LINE ▶▶▶▶

July 1212

Both ends of London Bridge catch on fire, making it impossible to escape.

2 September 1666

The Great Fire of London begins in a bakery.

Where is London?

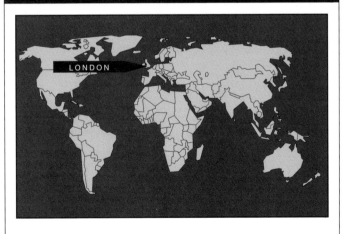

LONDON

DID YOU KNOW? ▶▶▶

During the Great Fire, people tried to stop the flames by destroying their houses. This way, the fire would not have anything to burn.

KEY TERMS ▶▶▶

thatch roof
> a house covering made of straw

firebreak
> a strip of land cleared to stop a fire

plague
> a disease that spreads quickly and causes death

Chapter 2   London, 1212, 1666

Many European cities grew up around rivers. Boats moved up and down these rivers long before there were cars or trains.

The Thames River runs through London, England. London is a very old city. Many of London's beautiful buildings and bridges are hundreds of years old.

London Bridge was built in the 1170s. This bridge was more than just a way to cross the Thames River. It became a kind of neighbourhood.

Hundreds of families lived in houses built on the bridge. There were many shops on the bridge, too. Thousands of people used the London Bridge every day. It was a very busy place.

London Bridge Is on Fire!

One windy day in July 1212, London Bridge caught fire. Both ends of the bridge were burning. People on the bridge were trapped. The wind blew the fire toward the centre of the bridge.

Buildings on the bridge caught fire. The bridge's narrow street filled with smoke and flames. People panicked. Some jumped off the bridge.

About 3000 people died from the London Bridge fire. Many were burnt or crushed to death. Some drowned in the Thames River below.

All the houses on the bridge were destroyed. But parts of the bridge survived the fire. The huge stone piers were left. People could still use the bridge. It remained an important crossing for another 600 years.

Fighting Fires Without Water

There were no water hoses back in the Middle Ages when the London Bridge fire occurred. People used buckets of water to put out fires. But this did not work for very big fires.

Houses were made of wood with thatch roofs. Wood and dry straw burn quickly and easily. Once a fire started, it was difficult to control. Entire streets could go up in flames.

People tried to stop fires from spreading. They worked together to pull down houses. They used large hooks attached to long poles and chains.

This made a firebreak. They hoped the fire would not be able to cross the big gap they created. If they were lucky, the fire would burn itself out.

Unfortunately, this did not work in 1212. The London Bridge fire spread through the city. Most of London burnt to the ground.

London introduced new fire laws after the 1212 disaster. People built roofs using stone tiles instead of straw. Every neighbourhood had to keep its own hooks for pulling down buildings in an emergency.

The Great Fire of London, 1666

The Great Fire of London was not nearly so deadly as the London Bridge fire. Fewer than ten people died in the 1666 blaze.

The fire started in a bakery. The baker did not put out the fire in the oven before he went to bed. His shop caught fire. The flames spread.

It became a huge fire that burnt through London. Thousands of homes were destroyed. Churches and other buildings were ruined. The Great Fire burned down entire neighbourhoods.

There were many rats. Rats carried germs that made people sick.

The year before the Great Fire, a terrible plague had killed thousands. The Great Fire of London killed a lot of the rats causing the plague.

After the fire, people rebuilt houses. The streets of London were cleaner than before. There were far fewer rats and less disease after the Great Fire of London.

Ocean liner passes under the Tower Bridge.

DATAFILE

TIME LINE ▶▶▶

1930

A luxury cruise ship named *Morro Castle* is built.

8 September 1934

A mysterious fire starts in the library on the *Morro Castle* cruise ship on its way back to New York.

Where is New York?

KEY TERMS ▶▶▶

luxury
> giving a feeling of comfort

Great Depression
> a period in the 1930s when many people did not have jobs

smuggling
> the practice of carrying something illegal into or out of a country

fireproof
> made so that it does not burn

Chapter 3   The *Morro Castle*, 1934

The *Morro Castle* was a luxury cruise ship. It was built in 1930. It sailed between New York and Havana, Cuba.

Hundreds of people enjoyed a floating holiday aboard the *Morro Castle*. They ate the finest food. They danced to music played by a live band. But the last voyage of the ship was a horror.

The history of the *Morro Castle* reads like a mystery story. And the mystery of the *Morro Castle* has never been solved.

The Great Depression

It cost a lot to travel to Cuba and back on the *Morro Castle*. Most people did not have enough money to go on the *Morro Castle*.

The 1930s were a difficult time for the world. It was the Great Depression. The stockmarket crashed. People lost their savings. Many people were out of work.

Those lucky to have jobs had to settle for very little money. Most people were struggling. But some rich people still had money to spend. And sailing on the *Morro Castle* was one way for them to escape the Great Depression for a few days and have fun.

However, the crew was not having fun. They were paid very little money to work on the ship. The crew was given bad food while the passengers feasted.

Some of the *Morro Castle* crew tried to make extra money by smuggling. They got things in Cuba and hid them on the ship to take back to the United States to sell.

The crew even smuggled people into America on board the *Morro Castle*. They could make a lot of money this way. But it was against the law. If they were caught, they would go to jail.

The captain of the *Morro Castle* tried to keep order on ship. It was a difficult job. And the crew hated the captain for doing it.

The Captain Is Dead!

Friday 7 September 1934 was the last night of the cruise. The *Morro Castle* was due back in New York at eight o'clock the next morning.

It was time for dinner. But the captain was not at his table. One of the crew went to look for him. He found the captain dead.

Was the captain murdered? No-one knew for sure. He may have had a heart attack. There were rumours that he was poisoned. But even today his death is a mystery.

Fire!

The chief officer took over the *Morro Castle*. His name was William Warms. Warms was second in command. Now that the captain was dead, it was his job to get the ship safely back to New York. Unfortunately, he was not good at his job.

A fire started in the ship's library. No-one knows for sure how the fire began. It might have been an accident. Someone might have dropped a lighted cigarette. Or the fire might have been set on purpose. The cause of the fire is one more part of this unsolved mystery.

One of the crew told Warms about the fire. Warms was not worried about the fire. The *Morro Castle* was supposed to be fireproof! Warms didn't even try to put out the fire. This was a big mistake.

There was a storm that night. Chief Officer Warms was more worried about the storm than the fire. He was not used to sailing the ship. He was in a hurry to get back to New York. The *Morro Castle* sailed for New York at top speed.

The winds from the storm fanned the fire in the library. More and more books caught fire. The flames spread. Soon the whole ship was on fire. The fire was out of control. Now there was no way to put it out.

The firefighting equipment did not work. There was no water running to the fire hoses up on deck. Were they just broken? Or had someone turned them off on purpose? This was another mystery, like the death of the captain.

By this time it was around three o'clock in the morning. Most of the passengers were sleeping. No-one sounded an alarm.

The crew took the lifeboats for themselves instead of doing their jobs and waking the sleeping passengers. Six lifeboats carried 85 people safely away from the burning ship. Only 5 of the 85 were passengers. The rest were crew, including officers.

The *Morro Castle* was only a few kilometres from shore. But it never made it back to New York; 134 of the 549 people on board died.

The End of the *Morro Castle*

The *Morro Castle* sank just off the coast of New Jersey, close to a hotel. People could see the burning ship from the shore.

A large crowd gathered on the beach. Some people started selling ice-cream and hot dogs as they watched the end of this disaster.

Word of the disaster spread. More and more people came to see for themselves. By that afternoon, a quarter of a million people had turned up. The army was called in to move the crowd away.

The burnt-out shell of the ship became a tourist attraction. People bought tickets to see the place where all those people died.

It's Still a Mystery

William Warms and some of the other officers were sentenced to jail. They should have done more to save the passengers. They were partly to blame for the disaster. But the mystery of the captain's death was never solved.

TIME LINE ▶▶▶

1869

The Chicago Water Tower is built. It becomes one of the only buildings to survive the fire.

8 October 1871

The Great Fire of Chicago begins in a barn.

Where is Chicago?

DID YOU KNOW?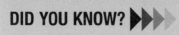

The Great Fire of Chicago started in the O'Leary barn. Even though the fire destroyed much of the city, the O'Leary house was not burnt.

KEY TERMS ▶▶▶▶

lantern
> a light inside a glass or paper case

historian
> an expert in history

mill
> a building where grain is ground into flour or meal

Chapter 4   Chicago, 1871

The Great Fire of Chicago started as a small barn fire. It began around 9 pm on Sunday 8 October 1871.

By midnight, much of the city was on fire. Firefighters worked all night to control the fire. Rain started to fall two days later. This helped put out the last of the flames.

When it was all over, 300 people were dead and 90 000 were left homeless. More than 7.5 square kilometres of the city were in ruins. The fire destroyed property worth almost $200 million.

Mrs O'Leary's Cow

A popular song blames the Chicago fire on a woman milking her cow.

'One dark night, when people were in bed,

Mrs O'Leary lit a lantern in her shed,

The cow kicked it over, winked its eye, and said,

"There'll be a hot time in the old town tonight".'

Historians doubt that this was really how the fire started. But they do agree that it started in Mrs O'Leary's barn.

How did an ordinary barn fire turn into the Great Fire of Chicago? From the beginning, everything went wrong.

Firefighters were already very tired from fighting another big fire the previous night. That fire had started in a mill Saturday evening.

The firefighters were up all Saturday night and through to Sunday afternoon. Many of them had not eaten or slept when they heard that the O'Leary's barn was on fire.

The fire engines and equipment were not ready to fight another big fire so soon either. One of the fire engines broke down. Some of the fire hoses were not working well.

Another problem was that the fire was not reported right away. Then the firefighters went to the wrong place. By the time the firefighters arrived at the barn, the fire was already out of control.

If the firefighters had reached the fire earlier, they could have put it out quickly.

The barn was full of hay and coal. Both burnt and made the fire very big and very hot. The wind spread the fire.

Was the Cow to Blame?

Mrs O'Leary said she did not cause the fire. She and her husband said they were asleep in bed when the fire started. They were probably telling the truth.

If Mrs O'Leary had been in the barn when the fire started she could have put it out. At least she would have run to get help right away. She would have wanted to save her barn, her animals and her milk business.

So then how did this story get started? A Chicago newspaper reported that a cow had kicked over a lamp. Straw on the floor of the barn caught fire, then the barn itself, and eventually the city.

Peg-Leg Daniel Sullivan

A key suspect was Daniel Sullivan. Daniel Sullivan had a drinking problem. He lived near the O'Learys. He may have started the fire when he was smoking in the barn.

Daniel refused to take the blame for the fire. He told this incredible story instead. He said he was across the road when he saw the flames. He ran into the barn to save a calf.

His wooden leg got stuck in a crack in the floor. He had to take it off to escape. He hopped out clinging to the neck of a rescued calf.

The City Rebuilds

Chicago was rebuilt after the fire. Like London after their Great Fire, the new city of Chicago was safer and more beautiful. Today little evidence of the disastrous fire remains. But people do still occasionally sing the song.

'One dark night, when people were in bed,

Mrs O'Leary lit a lantern in her shed,

The cow kicked it over, winked its eye, and said,

"There'll be a hot time in the old town tonight".'

The city of Chicago in ruins after the Great Fire of 1871

The Chicago skyline today

DATAFILE

TIME LINE ▶▶▶▶

18 November 1903

> The United States and Panama sign a treaty to build the Panama Canal.

30 December 1903

> Iroquois Theatre in Chicago goes up in flames during a play.

Where is Panama?

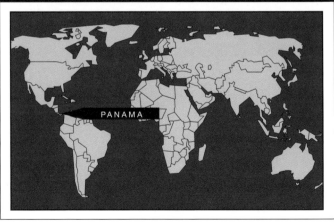

PANAMA

KEY TERMS ▶▶▶▶

intermission
> a break between two acts of a
> play

scenery
> a painted backdrop used on the
> stage of a play

canvas
> a heavy cloth used for painting

Chapter 5   Iroquois Theatre, 1903

Some disasters seem more tragic than others. The 1903 Iroquois Theatre fire was especially sad. Many of the victims were children and their mothers.

It was 30 December. Schools were closed for the holidays. That afternoon's show was sold out.

More than 1900 people crowded into the six-storey theatre. They were there to see a musical comedy. There would be singing and dancing. They were looking forward to a fun time.

Instead, it turned into a horrible nightmare.

Theatre Fires

There had been many tragic theatre fires before. Theatre fires were a big problem in the United States and Europe.

Most fires started high above the stage. Theatres have lots of lights near the ceiling. These lights shine on the actors on stage. They are very bright. And they can get very hot.

There was also a lot of painted scenery above the stage. During the show, the old scenery was pulled up. New scenery came down. Sometimes the scenery accidentally touched these hot lights. The paint on the canvas burnt easily.

By 1903, theatres kept firefighters near the stage, just in case. New theatres also had to have a fireproof curtain.

If a fire broke out, the curtain would come down quickly. This kept the fire from spreading into the audience.

The Iroquois was a new theatre. It had just opened about a month before. It should have had the newest fire safety equipment. But it didn't. And what was there didn't work properly.

In 1903, the Iroquois Theatre was a disaster waiting to happen.

Fire! Fire!

It was about 3.15 in the afternoon. A fire started just after intermission. Everyone was back in their seats for the second half of the show. Some of the actors were on stage. The band was playing.

The fire started small. A piece of canvas brushed against a light high above the stage. A worker up there saw the tiny flame. He tried to crush it with his hand. But it was just out of reach.

The fire spread quickly. A light crashed down to the stage. The star of the show looked up and saw the fire. He told people not to panic. He urged them to stay in their seats. The band continued to play.

There was a fireman on duty. But he didn't have good equipment. He had only a small amount of powder for sprinkling on flames to put them out.

The powder didn't work. There were no fire hoses. There was no way to put out the fire.

The curtain never reached the floor. It got stuck on its way down. Some survivors said it caught fire. Maybe the workers lowered the wrong curtain.

Some of the burning scenery fell onto the singers and dancers. They rushed from the stage. There were about 500 people working behind the scenes. Almost all of them got out alive. They ran out a door behind the stage. But the tightrope walker stuck high above the stage died.

The blast of cold air from that open door blew the fire into the audience. Flames and smoke whipped through the seating area and up into the balcony.

Children cried out for their mothers. Mothers screamed for their children. The audience panicked. The lights had gone out. No-one could see in the smoky darkness.

There were iron gates over many of the exit doors. Some of these gates were locked. Others were hard to open.

Many of the doors opened inwards. People were already pressed against the doors. There was no way to open these doors either. The only way out was through the main doors.

About two-thirds of the audience managed to escape. They were the lucky ones.

In only 15 minutes, 600 people were dead. Many were trapped behind doors that would not open. Some of them were still in their seats.

Life Goes On

The Fire Department arrived. They quickly put out the fire. The theatre was not badly damaged. It reopened less than a year later. But it changed its name to the Colonial Theatre. It was torn down in 1925 to make room for a new theatre.

TIME LINE

December 1993 – January 1994

More than 800 fires threaten
Sydney, Australia

25 December 2001

Bushfires rage near Sydney.

Where is Sydney?

SYDNEY

KEY TERMS ▶▶▶▶

bush

        wild land in the countryside

Equator

        an imaginary line around the middle of the Earth. It is equal distance from North and South Pole.

rage

        to be out of control

Chapter 6   Australian Bushfires, 2001

Sydney, Australia was home to the 2000 Olympics. The Games were a great success. Millions of people around the world saw this beautiful city on television.

In 2001 this same city faced disaster. Fires broke out in the 'bush', or countryside, near the city. These fires, called bushfires, were closing in on Sydney. Smoke filled the sky and blocked the sun. Many people were forced to leave their homes. It was too dangerous for them to stay.

Summer Christmas

The fires started on Christmas Day. Australia is south of the Equator. When it's winter in the Northern Hemisphere, it's summer in Australia. Australian summers are hot and dry. Australia has many bushfires in November, December and January. But not all of these turn into disasters.

Thousands of firefighters spent Christmas Day battling the blazes instead of opening presents with their families. Strong winds made it very difficult to control the fires. Firefighters from other parts of Australia came to help. About 22 000 firefighters were on the ground and in the air fighting the fire. Water was dropped from aeroplanes and helicopters.

The fires raged for two weeks. More than half a million hectares of bushland burnt. About 170 properties were lost.

This was not the first time Christmas fires had threatened Sydney. More than 800 fires started between 27 December 1993 and 16 January 1994.

December 1997 brought even worse fires to the city. Fires raged in bushland on three sides of Sydney.

But the 2001 Sydney bushfires may not have been an accident. Police suspected that arsonists might have started many of them. Arsonists set fires on purpose. A special arson squad, Strikeforce Tronto, worked to find the arsonists.

Police arrested more than 20 suspects. Most were between nine and 16 years old. A new plan required children guilty of arson to meet hospital patients with severe burns. This way, they would see the result of their crimes. Adults were sentenced to up to 14 years in prison.

Volunteer Firefighters

Australia has thousands of volunteer firefighters. These brave men and women risk their lives for no pay. They have other regular jobs they do most days. Some work in shops or banks. Some are teachers. They risk their lives fighting fires because they care about helping other people. Many of them feel that this is the most important thing they do. Thanks to their efforts, Australia has lost very few lives to bushfires.

Australian firefighters travel to other countries, including the United States, to teach others what they do. Not only do they save lives in their own country, their experience and know-how help save lives all over the world.

TIME LINE ▶▶▶

17 February 2003

A stampede erupts in a Chicago nightclub.

20 February 2003

Fire breaks out at The Station nightclub in Rhode Island.

Where is Rhode Island?

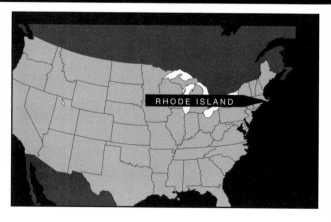

RHODE ISLAND

DID YOU KNOW? ▶▶▶▶

The Station was a small wooden building. It was not required to have a sprinkler system because it was built before 1976.

KEY TERMS ▶▶▶▶

heavy metal

a kind of music that is heavy on bass, guitar and drums

foam

a soft, sponge-like material

About 100 people died when a fire broke out at a club in West Warwick, Rhode Island, USA. It was one of the worst club fires in recent history. A heavy metal band was playing at The Station nightclub. They set off sparklers at the start of their show. Sparks flew everywhere. Some of them hit soft foam on the walls. This started a fire. Thick, poisonous smoke from the burning foam filled the club.

The club was on fire! People panicked. They raced for exits. Every second counts during a club fire. Too many people and too few exits is a deadly combination. The band's speakers blocked one of the emergency exits near the stage. Most of the people tried to get out the front doors.

Some of the dead burnt to death. Others died from breathing the fire's poisonous smoke. Some may have been crushed to death in the rush to escape the burning building. One of the dead was a member of the band that was playing that night. Some of the dead bodies were so badly burnt they could not be identified.

About 180 survivors were very badly burnt, too. Some of them had no skin left on their faces.

This disaster made people more aware of the danger of club fires. Fire inspectors have closed several clubs since The Station fire. Those clubs were not safe. One of them might have been the next club fire disaster.

The Cocoanut Grove Fire: Boston, 1942

This deadly fire started small, too. Someone at the nightclub took a light bulb out of its socket. He wanted his corner of the room darker. A young waiter went to put a light bulb back in. He lit a match to see where it went. The flame touched one of the fake palm trees. It caught fire. The fire spread to other fake palm trees. Silk curtains turned into sheets of flames.

The club was full of people. They panicked. Everyone rushed to the exits. But emergency doors had been bolted shut. Others were hidden behind curtains. People didn't know they were there.

The only way out was a very slow revolving door. When firefighters arrived, they broke down the revolving door. They found a heap of dead bodies piled six-deep behind it.

There were 900 people in the club that night. About half of them died in the fire.

The Cinq-Sept Club Fire: France, 1970

Sometimes it takes a disaster to get people to make changes. After the Boston Cocoanut Grove club fire, American clubs became safer. There were more fire exits. Unfortunately, other countries did not learn from the Cocoanut Grove tragedy.

On 1 November 1970, a popular band was playing at a nightclub in France. Two hundred fans packed the club. The club did not want people sneaking in without paying. So they locked all the emergency doors. There was only one way in and out of the club.

Someone dropped a lighted match. It landed on a cushion. The cushion caught fire. Flames shot up the plastic sheets. In less than a minute, the hall was on fire. Black smoke filled the club.

The smoke from the burning plastic was poisonous. People could not see or breathe. About 150 people died instantly. Some ran to the exit. But the turnstile jammed. Only 60 people escaped.

Epilogue

There are different kinds of firefighters for different kinds of fires. Smokejumpers fight forest fires.

Smokejumpers take a plane into the air. Then they jump from the plane using a parachute. The parachute lands them safely on the ground.

Sometimes smokejumpers carry small tanks of water on their backs. They also carry supplies. Altogether, their load could weigh 45 kilograms!

Sometimes smokejumpers stay in the forest for weeks looking for places where another fire could start. A wildfire not only destroys the natural habitat, it could also destroy homes and other buildings. Smokejumpers want to stop fires before they get this far.

Bibliography

Balcavage, Dynise. *The great Chicago fire.* Great Disasters, Reforms and Ramifications. Broomall, PA: Chelsea House Publishers, 2002.

Landau, Elaine. *Fires.* Watts Library. New York: Franklin Watts, 1999.

Shields, Charles J. *The great plague and fire of London.* Great Disasters, Reforms and Ramifications. Philadelphia: Chelsea House Publishers, 2002.

Thompson, Luke. *Forest fires.* High Interest Books. New York: Children's Press, 2000.

Index